Bird Life
in Hawaii

ANDREW J. BERGER

ISLAND 🌀 HERITAGE

Published by
Island Heritage

Forth Edition, 1986
Copyright © 1983 Island Heritage Limited
ALL RIGHTS RESERVED

Please address orders, editorial correspondence and
catalog requests to
Island Heritage
1819 Kahai Street
Honolulu, Hawaii 96819-3136
(808) 847-5566

Printed and bound in Hong Kong
Library of Congress Catalog number 83-081140
ISBN 0-89610-090-1

CREDITS

Photographs—
    Andrew J. Berger: pp. 10, 14-16, 50.

Illustrations—
    Sue Monden: Front and back covers, title page, pp. 11, 13,
            17, 25, 29, 43-49, 51-55, 57, 70.
    Barbara Downs: pp. 56, 68 (Yellow-billed Cardinal).
    Wilson & Evans: pp. 19, 24, 27, 30, 35, 38-39, 41.
    Rothschild: pp. 9, 20-23, 26, 28, 31-34, 36-37, 40.

Book design—
    Teresa Black

Contents

An Introduction

THE HAWAIIAN ISLANDS ENJOY a unique isolation in the middle of the Pacific Ocean some 2,400 miles from the continental land masses of North America and Asia. The island chain itself extends about 1,600 miles from the island of Hawaii in the southeast to Kure Atoll in the northwest. The Islands, entirely volcanic in origin, were formed by molten magma that poured out of fissures in the ocean floor. After millions of years the submarine mountains that were formed pushed their peaks high above the ocean and the Hawaiian Islands were born. The process still continues.

No one knows, of course, when the molten lava of the first island cooled, when the first plants began to grow there, or when the first birds reached that island. There seems little doubt, however, that the first birds to reach the newly formed Hawaiian Islands were sea birds. Such birds, flying over the unmarked expanses of the ocean throughout much of the year, undoubtedly were the earliest residents. At some unknown time, land birds also found their way to one or more of the Islands. They were probably blown off course by the high winds that accompany widespread storms.

A pair of birds or a small flock could have established a colonizing population if the island provided food, shelter and safe breeding places.

The successful colonization of places like the Hawaiian Islands which are located so far from continents is uncommon. Only rarely are the combination of factors just right—viz., birds in the right places at the right times, with the storm winds or jet streams blowing in the right direction—even for the birds to reach the Hawaiian Islands. It would be more rare for such windblown birds to find suitable living conditions when they did reach the Islands. For example, about 120 species of birds have been recorded as stragglers to the Hawaiian Islands during the past 100 years. Some of these birds have been seen only once, but others repeatedly find their way to Hawaii. At least 11 species of gulls have been reported in the Hawaiian Islands one or more times, and yet no species of gull has become established as a breeding bird; the gulls are seen for a few days or weeks, and then they disappear. We do not know whether they move on, or whether they do not find adequate food and die.

And yet, the Hawaiian Islands do have winter residents, birds that nest in Alaska or Siberia and that spend the nonbreeding period in the Islands. Among the most common of these winter residents are the Pintail, Shoveler, Lesser Scaup, Bristle-thighed Curlew, Wandering Tattler, Ruddy Turnstone, Sanderling and Pacific Golden Plover. Adult plovers reach the Islands in August, juvenile birds several weeks later. In Hawaii the plovers inhabit city lawns, golf courses, pastures, cutover sugar cane fields and open areas up to elevations of 10,000 feet on the island of Hawaii. Flocks of turnstones and sanderlings are readily seen at Kanaha Pond on Maui.

Since 1778, when Captain James Cook discovered the Sandwich Islands (as he named them), ornithologists have found 70 different kinds of birds unlike any to be found in any other parts of the world.

The 70 kinds of endemic Hawaiian birds developed from only 15 different ancestral populations. Over long periods of time some of the ancestral birds gave rise to several species (or different kinds) of birds as a result of the unique conditions found in Hawaii. Such an evolutionary process is referred to as adaptive radiation or evolutionary divergence. For example, the offspring from an ancestral population could move into unoccupied habitats and niches, such as marshes, dry forests, or mountain rain forests. In the rain forests, the birds might adapt to feeding in the crowns of trees towering 100 feet into the sky, or they might

5

prefer to live primarily in the understory. Living and feeding in these new settings slowly altered the genes of the birds. Such mutations were manifested in different kinds of bills, tongues and other anatomical features. In time there evolved species of birds that were unlike their ancestral population and different from any in the world. Ornithologists refer to these unique birds as endemic.

The native species that inhabit the Hawaiian Islands can be grouped as sea birds or oceanic birds, pond and marsh birds, and true land birds. Sea birds, such as the Laysan Albatross, the Red-tailed Tropicbird and the Sooty Tern spend much of their life flying over the open ocean. Typically, these birds come to the Islands only during the nesting season.

Hawaii's pond and marsh birds include the Nene or Hawaiian Goose (the state bird), the Koloa or Hawaiian Duck, the Laysan . Duck, the Black-crowned Night Heron, the Hawaiian Coot, the Hawaiian Gallinule and the Hawaiian Black-necked Stilt. Of these, the Nene shows the greatest changes from its ancestral species and relatives in other parts of the world. Unlike other species of geese, the Nene has adapted for living in a rugged habitat of lava far from any running or standing water. Few, if any, wild Nene ever swim, and these birds have the least webbing between their toes of any geese. Today the Nene are to be found primarily at elevations between about 5,000 and 8,000 feet on Mauna Loa and Hualalai on the island of Hawaii.

By the time Captain Cook discovered the Islands, the true endemic land birds were a hawk, an owl, a crow, two thrushes, an Old World warbler, an Old World flycatcher, five species of Old World honeyeaters and one entire family of Hawaiian honeycreepers (*Drepanididae*). The family Drepanididae, with its 28 species of birds, demonstrates the results of adaptive radiation much more strikingly than any other of the world's 170 bird families.

Of the 70 different kinds of unique Hawaiian birds, almost 40 percent are now thought to be extinct (Table 1) and another 50 percent are classified by the United States Fish and Wildlife Service as threatened or endangered (Table 2). The latter account for about one half of all the birds listed in the Red Book of endangered North American birds. It is tragic that so many beautiful and unique creatures are lost to us forever.

The Polynesians are thought to have colonized the Hawaiian Islands about 1,000 years ago. We can only imagine what the Islands were like then. We do know that most of the flowers, trees, and fruits that we associate with Honolulu and other lowland areas today were lacking. These were introduced after Captain Cook came to the Islands.

There were marshes and ponds in the lowlands, including what is now Waikiki, where gallinules, coots, stilts and the Hawaiian Duck were common throughout the year, and where thousands of migratory ducks from Alaska and Siberia spent the winter months.

Most of the mountains surely were covered by forests of endemic plants such as koa, ohia and sandalwood trees, and in the wetter areas, giant tree ferns and many other species of moisture-loving plants. The endemic birds filled these forests, feeding on the flowers of the ohia, koa and mamane trees or on insects and seeds. Although it seems logical to assume that these birds had some parasites, they had no mammalian predators: no dogs, cats, rats, or mongooses.

And, as we see today, there were areas covered by barren lava flows, as on the islands of Hawaii and Maui.

Anthropologists tell us that the Polynesians brought with them a wide variety of plants, jungle fowl, pigs, dogs and, presumably accidentally, the Polynesian rat (*Rattus exulans*). The extent to which the pigs, dogs and rats preyed upon the native birds is unknown, but it is reasonable to assume that they did, and that the pigs rooted up and destroyed vast areas of the rich forest floor just as they do today.

The Hawaiians ate young and adult sea birds that nested on the main islands and on the small offshore islands. David Malo, "the great authority and repository of Hawaiian lore," wrote that the Hawaiians also ate Bulwer's Petrel, Hawaiian Stilt, Golden

Plover, Bristle-thighed Curlew, Coot, Hawaiian Rail, Crow, 'Elepaio, Mamo, 'Amakihi and other endemic birds.

We can be certain that the Hawaiians killed untold thousands of the small and colorful endemic forest birds for their feathers, to make capes and headdresses for the chiefs. For example, curators at the Bernice P. Bishop Museum have estimated that about 500,000 yellow feathers from 80,000 Mamo (*Drepanis pacifica*) were used to make the spectacular feather cape of Kamehameha the Great, which is now displayed there. And, when Captain Cook first landed on Kauai on January 20, 1778, the natives brought to him "great numbers of skins of small red birds," tied in bundles of 20 or more or held together by a skewer run through their nostrils.

The serious degradation of the unique Hawaiian flora and fauna, however, began only a few years after Captain Cook first discovered the Islands: He and later ships' captains released cattle, horses, sheep, goats and English pigs to roam free. The ships' captains wanted to insure a supply of meat for their subsequent stops at the Islands. The earth "had been created for man's use," and the word "ecology" was not to be coined by German biologist Ernst Haeckel until 1869; as a field of science, ecology dates back only to about 1900.

When Captain Vancouver brought a second load of cattle to the island of Hawaii in 1794, he asked King Kamehameha to proclaim a 10-year kapu on the cattle and other introduced European mammals so that the common people could not kill them. King Kamehameha granted Vancouver's request, and the captain wrote that observance of such a 10-year kapu could "not fail to render the extirpation of these animals a task not easily to be accomplished." Vancouver was correct, of course, and to this day, goats, pigs, sheep and axis deer continue to destroy the vegetation on most of the Islands.

With the destruction of the native vegetation in the lowlands, first for the cultivation of taro and sweet potatoes by the Hawaiians and later for the cultivation of sugar cane and pineapple by other immigrants to Hawaii, the endemic forest birds became restricted to the high valleys and the mountains. Except in the marshes and ponds near sea level, where ducks, coots, gallinules, herons and stilts were common, there were virtually no birds at all in the lowland areas throughout most of the year. Not until the migrant Golden Plover and other shore birds returned to Hawaii in late summer were birds to be seen by most people.

Writing about his experiences from 1823 to 1825, missionary C. S. Stewart complained about Honolulu and Waikiki that "the mountains are too distant to be reached in an hour's ramble; and the shore is lined only with fishponds and marshes. There is not a tree near us, much less groves, in whose shade we might find shelter from the heat of the torrid sun; no babbling brooks, no verdant lawn, no secluded dell or glade, for the enjoyment of solitude and thought; indeed nothing that ever formed part of a scene of rural delight."

The editor of *The Polynesian*, a newspaper, wrote on October 17, 1840: "The broad avenues which now intersect the town [Honolulu], will become eventually fine streets. If they could be lined with trees, it would add much to the comfort of the pedestrian." Since that time more than 4,500 species of exotic flowers, shrubs and trees have been brought to Hawaii. Thus, with the notable exceptions of the coconut palm and the beach naupaka, virtually every plant that characterizes today's tropical "Hawaiian paradise" is a foreign plant.

The new residents in Hawaii must have missed the songbirds or garden birds, because one finds such pleas as appeared in *The Commercial Advertiser* for August 15, 1860: "Owners of vessels leaving foreign ports for Honolulu, will confer a great favor by sending out birds, when it can be done without great expense. We need more songsters here."

Well-to-do persons living here imported and released large numbers of foreign birds during the last century and in the early part of this century. In 1930 a group of kamaaina formed the Hui Manu or "bird society," whose sole aim was to introduce songbirds to Hawaii. It was the hope of the Hui Manu that the introduced birds would flourish and add both color and song to the gardens and heavily vegetated areas in such places as Manoa Valley, Nuuanu Valley and the Tantalus region of Honolulu. Some 20 species had been imported by the Hui Manu by 1942. More than 170 species of foreign birds have been released in Hawaii since the first Common Pigeons were reportedly imported in 1796. These include at least 78 kinds of gamebirds, many of which were introduced by the State Division of Fish and Game between 1949 and 1966. Of these, 53 were gallinaceous birds (quail, francolin, partridges, pheasants) and 20 were columbiform birds (pigeons and doves). The rest were an odd assortment, from the Chinese Fishing Cormorant to the Guam Cave Swiftlet, and a wide variety of passerine birds.

Of the 170 species that gained their freedom in Hawaii, about 50 species have become established. Several kinds are so recent that it remains to be seen if they will survive. Past experience has shown that a species may establish a small breeding population but it later dies out. For example, more than 100 Orange-breasted Buntings were released on Oahu between 1941 and 1950, and those birds were said to be nesting in Manoa Valley. However, none of these birds have been seen for more than 30 years, so it is reasonable to assume that the species did not survive.

1. Sea Birds

SEA BIRDS OR OCEANIC BIRDS belong to several orders and families of birds. Offshore species are associated with continents and they are most common in regions that have an extensive continental shelf. These birds share a common feature with the pelagic species in that both typically come to land only during their breeding season. Many of these sea birds have a long life span (30 years or more) and they may not reach breeding age for five years or longer. The immature, nonbreeding birds may remain at sea throughout the year, some flying thousands of miles from their nesting site. The 22 kinds of oceanic birds found in the Hawaiian Islands belong to three orders and seven families of birds.

In addition to fishes, sea birds feed on squid and a wide variety of Crustacea and other animal life found in the plankton near the surface of the water. Fresh water is unavailable at most sites where sea birds nest, and, in fact, sea birds can drink salt water because of special glands, located above the eyes, that secrete a fluid having a higher concentration of salts than does the sea water.

Most sea birds lay a single egg, often white, but sometimes speckled with small spots of reddish, brown, or lavender colors. Most also lay their eggs on the ground or in burrows in the ground; a few build nests in shrubs or trees. The Hawaiian summer sun is exceedingly hot, especially on offshore islands and on the sand and coral islands in the Leeward chain. Nesting adults therefore encounter the problem of excessive heat and solar radiation not only for themselves but also for the eggs or newly hatched young. Hence, the adults often have to stand over the egg or young in order to provide shade for it. Both adult and young birds cool themselves by evaporative cooling, either by panting or by gular fluttering—that is, by rapidly vibrating the throat and floor of the mouth, thus speeding up blood flow and loss of heat through the moist lining membranes.

Laysan Albatross, *Diomedea immutabilis*. (Illustration on previous page.)

This large, trim, black-and-white bird is about 32 inches long and weighs five to seven pounds. Long known as Gooney birds by sailors, this albatross now apparently nests only in the Hawaiian Islands. The population on Laysan Island has been estimated at half-a-million birds. Laysan Albatrosses first nested near Kilauea Point, Kauai, during 1977; ten birds were found at Barking Sands the following year. Wild dogs, however, killed seven of the adult birds.

Many Laysan Albatrosses do not breed until they are eight or nine years old. By studying banded birds, we now know that some birds live as long as 42 years. Albatrosses have elaborate courtship displays accompanied by vocalizations and bill-snapping. Both the male and the female form a nest depression. The female lays a single dull-white egg. Most of the eggs on Laysan Island are laid during November and December. Both sexes take turns in incubating the egg for a period averaging 64.5 days. Two to six days may be required for the young chick to break its way out of the eggshell. Both adults bring food to the young, which are able to fly when they are 165 days old.

Wedge-tailed Shearwater or 'Ua'u Kani, *Puffinus pacificus chlororbyncbus*. (Above.)

This shearwater has two color phases: Dark-phase birds are almost entirely dark, sooty brown; light-phase birds have white underparts. Nearly all of the birds in the Hawaiian Islands have the white underparts. The species is widespread, nesting on islands throughout most of the tropical Pacific Ocean and in the Indian Ocean. The birds are common during the summer months on Rabbit Island off the Windward coast of Oahu and several thousand nest at Kilauea Point, Kauai. During the daytime before the single egg is laid, the two adults often sit quietly together near the nest site. Beginning shortly after dusk, however, the birds begin to emit a wide variety of moans, groans and wails, as do many other species of petrels and shearwaters. Hence they sometimes are called the "moaning" birds. Both adults share incubation duties and feeding of the nestling, by regurgitation. The eggs hatch during August on Rabbit Island. The adult shearwaters leave the nesting islands about two weeks before the young birds are ready to fly. During this period the young live on stored fat and exercise their wings.

White-tailed Tropicbird or Koaʻe Kea, *Phaethon lepturus dorotheae*.

Tropicbirds are primarily white birds with a pair of highly specialized inner tail feathers that are narrow and greatly elongated. These unfeatherlike feathers are called streamers. Sometimes called the Yellow-billed Tropicbird because of its yellow bill, this species has a wide distribution in the tropical Pacific Ocean. In Hawaii the birds are usually restricted to the main islands, rarely occurring in the Leeward chain of islands. The birds are especially noticeable in Waimea Canyon on Kauai, on the Windward side of the Pali on Oahu and inside Kilauea Crater at

Volcanoes National Park on Hawaii. A single egg is laid on the ground; no nest is made. The egg has a chalky white to creamy base-color and the shell is heavily spotted with various shades of reddish-brown, purplish-red, etc. The Hawaiian race usually nests on cliffs, but other subspecies nest in trees. Both parents feed the young by regurgitation. The chicks become fully feathered at 40 days of age but they are not able to fly until more than 60 days of age. Tropicbirds have fully webbed feet, so that they are clumsy on the ground. Once airborne, however, tropicbirds are exceedingly graceful. They feed primarily on fish and squid, often hovering over the prey before diving headfirst into the water. Sailors call these birds Bo'sunbirds.

Red-footed Booby or ʻĀ, *Sula sula rubripes*. (Illustration on title page.)

This is the smallest of the three species of boobies that occur in Hawaiian waters. The total length of the bird is about 28 inches and the wingspan about 40 inches. Boobies were so named by sailors many years ago because the birds showed little or no fear of men and could easily be grabbed from a ship's rigging; to some, they also looked and acted stupid. In addition to their distribution throughout much of the tropical Pacific, the Red-footed Booby nests on nearly all of the Leeward Islands as well as at the Kilauea Point Lighthouse area of Kauai and the Mokapu Peninsula on Oahu. The latter colony is believed to have established itself about 1946. The Red-footed Booby apparently always builds its nest off of the ground, but this may be only a foot or so above the ground where the vegetation is low. New material is added to the nest during the incubation period. "Landing calls" and "stick-shake" displays accompany the return to the nest and the nest-building activities. A single white egg with a chalky outer coat is laid. The skin of the newly hatched chick has various shades of purplish-pink. By the time the chick is a little more than two weeks old, it is covered by a fluffy coat of white down. When a human intruder disturbs boobies at the nest, both the nestling and the adults tend to regurgitate their last meal, usually in the direction of, and sometimes on, the intruder. Boobies have been recaptured 20 years after they had been banded as nestlings.

Great Frigatebird or 'Iwa, *Fregata minor palmerstoni.*

Frigatebirds are very large birds, averaging 43 inches in length and having a wingspread of over seven feet. Females have a white throat and upper breast. The males have a highly inflatable, bare, red gular pouch that can be inflated at will during the breeding season, and the birds sometimes fly with the pouch fully inflated. The birds also are known as Man-o'-War birds because of their habit of harrassing boobies and other sea birds until they regurgitate their food in flight; the frigatebird then swoops down and catches the food before it hits the water. Frigatebirds build relatively frail, flat nests that are composed of twigs and branches. These birds are unusual in that the females presumably collect most of the nesting material and the males actually build the nest. Frigatebirds sometimes also rob twig-carrying boobies of their nesting material. Females lay a single white egg. Both adults take turns in incubating the egg. Frigatebirds nest on Kaula Island and on many of the Leeward Islands. Young birds do not come into breeding condition until about five years old. During their early years the birds wander widely over the Pacific, as far as the Philippines, and a population of 500 or more birds roosts on Moku Manu off the Windward coast of Oahu. Frigatebirds frequently soar over the coasts of Oahu and the drainage canal from Kawainui Swamp in Kailua. Banded birds are known to have reached an age of 34 years.

Sooty Tern or 'Ewa 'Ewa, *Sterna fuscata oahuensis.*

This is presumed to be the most abundant sea bird in the Pacific region. More than a million birds form some colonies. In Hawaii it nests on most of the Leeward Islands, on Moku Manu and Manana (Rabbit) Island. About 100,000 birds nest on Rabbit Island off the Windward coast of Oahu. The Sooty Tern is an important member of the mixed flocks of sea birds on which fishermen depend for locating schools of fish. In much of its range, the Sooty Tern is called the Wideawake Tern because of its incessant screeching, nerve-racking calls that are given both day and night. The Sooty Tern lays a single egg, the ground color varying from white to creamish-buff. There is a great variation in the markings on the eggs: Some have relatively fine, brownish markings whereas others have large splotches of burnt sienna brown. The two adults take turns incubating the egg. Most of the changeovers take place at night, but most of the eggs hatch during the daylight hours. As many as four days may be required for the young chicks to break out of the eggshell. At hatching the chicks have a full coat of down, the pattern being variegated with black, brown and white. As soon as the adults recognize their own chick, they will peck any foreign chick that strays close to the nest. Banded birds have been known to reach an age of 28 years.

Brown Noddy or Noio Kōhā, *Anous stolidus pileatus.*

This noddy has been found as a breeding bird on nearly all of the islands of the tropical Pacific Ocean. It nests on all of the islands of the Leeward chain and on Kaula, Moku Manu and Rabbit Island, as well as on a number of the smaller offshore islets. Some 30,000 birds nest on Rabbit Island, and some birds roost on the island year-round. Most of the egg-laying takes place in May and June. Pre-copulatory behavior includes preening of the female by the male and courtship feeding. In Hawaii most of the birds lay their eggs on bare ground or rock ledges. A pair may make no nest at all or may build a fairly bulky nest. The female lays a single egg that has a dull shell, typically having markings of small, brownish spots and dots sparsely scattered over the surface. The yolk in the Brown Noddy's egg is yellow, whereas that in the egg of the Sooty Tern is red to orange in color. The adults take turns in incubating the eggs; the average incubation period is 36 days. The chicks are notable because their full coat of down varies from black to white, with about half of the chicks having the dark coat. No one has been able to explain this difference in down color and all of the chicks molt into an identical immature plumage. During a two-year study on Rabbit Island more than 40 percent of the noddy chicks were killed by Black-crowned Night Herons. Brown Noddies may live as long as 25 years.

White Tern or Manu O Ku, *Gygis alba rothschildi*.

These small, graceful terns average 10 inches in length, with a wingspan of 28 inches. Their flight has been described as ethereal, with effortless wingbeats, although they sometimes seem to flutter erratically, especially as they hover over one's head. The White Tern also nests on most of the islands of the tropical Pacific, and they have nested on Oahu at least since 1961. They can be found at Koko Head, Kahala, Kapiolani Park, Fort DeRussy and near the police station and the Fernhurst YWCA on Punahou and Wilder. A single elliptical egg is laid. The ground color varies from grayish-white to creamy white, and the purple and brown markings consist of splotches, specks, lines, scrolls and scrawls, so there is great variation in the eggs of different females. No nest is built: On Oahu, and many other places, the egg usually is laid on a horizontal branch of a tree, sometimes 60 feet from the ground. The egg is incubated for 35 days, after which the white-to-tan downy chick must hold on to its branch for at least 40 days until it is able to fly. The adults dive to the surface of the water for fish but the birds do not submerge. The fish are carried crosswise in the bill as the adult returns to feed its nestling.

2. Native Water Birds

THESE ARE THREATENED SPECIES because of two primary factors: the destruction of their essential habitat and the presence of too many predators, such as mongooses, cats, dogs, rats, pigs, bullfrogs and large-mouthed bass. Long gone are the duck ponds of Waikiki and the tide pools and marshes where Ala Moana Shopping Center now stands. The very important Kaelepulu Pond is now Enchanted Lake; Salt Lake is no longer for the birds; and Kawainui Swamp is now nearly useless for the water birds, and will soon become so as the introduced plants clog up the last open water. The mammalian predators eat the eggs and young of the water birds and the bullfrogs and the bass also eat the young precocial chicks when they enter the water.

Five of the water birds are endemic to the Hawaiian Islands, whereas, although it is a permanent resident of the Islands, the Night Heron is considered indigenous because it has not been recognized as subspecifically different from Mainland populations.

Black-crowned Night Heron or 'Auku'u, *Nycticorax nycticorax boactli.*
(Illustration on previous page.)

The male and female are alike in breeding plumage, and it is during the nesting season that two or three long, highly modified, white nuptial plumes grow downward from the occipital (back) region of the head. The immature birds have a different plumage, being grayish-brown on the back, streaked with whitish and rusty hues; the underparts also are streaked with brownish and grayish feathers. Fully grown birds are about two feet long and have a wingspread of about 44 inches.

The 'Auku'u is found on all of the main islands, but is much reduced in numbers from earlier times. It inhabits ponds, marshes and lagoons, and many of these, as already noted, have been drained or filled. One of the largest populations is found at Kanaha Pond on Maui. The birds feed on aquatic insects, fish, frogs, mice and, at times, on chicks of the Sooty Tern, Brown Noddy and Hawaiian Stilt; although largely nocturnal, the birds also feed during the daytime. Herons build bulky nests of twigs and sticks in trees; in Hawaii the trees often are the introduced kiawe (mesquite) and ironwood (*Casuarina*). The eggs have a bluish-green shell, but little is known about the breeding biology of this heron in Hawaii. The 'Auku'u is mentioned in an ancient Hawaiian chant to Kualii, a chief noted for his bravery, strength and great desire for war.

Hawaiian Goose or Nene, *Branta sandvicensis*.

The Nene, an endangered species, is the state bird of Hawaii. It is a highly specialized goose with a considerable reduction of the webbing between its toes, adapted to living on rugged and sparsely vegetated lava flows at elevations above 4,000 feet on the island of Hawaii. There is no standing water on the lava flows and wild Nene never have an opportunity to swim, although they do so in captivity. A Nene Restoration Project has been under way at Pohakuloa on Hawaii since 1949 and at the Slimbridge Wildfowl Trust in England since 1951. More than 1,600 birds were raised at Pohakuloa and more than 1,500 of these birds had been released on Hawaii and in Haleakala Crater on Maui as of 1978; 197 birds from England also were released on Maui. During the nesting season from October to March, the Nene on Hawaii are confined to Mauna Loa and Hualalai Mountain. The eggs are immaculate, creamy white and the average clutch is 4.26 eggs, the number varying from three to six eggs. When she leaves the nest to feed, the goose covers the eggs with the downy feathers that she uses to line the nest. The incubation period is usually 30 days, and the precocial young are able to run about as soon as their down dries. The young are flightless for 10 to 12 weeks, however, and are then vulnerable to the predators that flourish in the Nene habitat. Volcanoes National Park and Haleakala National Park have Nene rearing programs, and Nene also can be seen at the Honolulu Zoo and at Waimea Falls Park on Oahu.

Hawaiian Duck or Koloa, *Anas wyvilliana*.

The Koloa is closely related to the common Mallard (*Anas platyrhynchos*) of North America, Europe and Asia, and hybridization in Hawaii is one of the dangers faced by the endemic Koloa. The speculum, the distinctive patch of bright feathers on the secondary wing feathers, varies from greenish to deep metallic purple in both sexes of the Koloa. Adult males vary from 19 to 20 inches in length; the females average about three inches shorter. The early range of the Koloa included all of the main islands except Lanai and Kahoolawe, but by 1915 the duck was considered rare except on Kauai. Charles W. Schwartz wrote that there were probably fewer than 30 birds remaining on Oahu in 1947; these were believed exterminated before 1960. A Koloa restoration program was initiated in 1962 with funds provided by the World Wildlife Fund and the Federal Aid to Wildlife Restoration Act. Nearly 300 ducks have been released on Hawaii and about 350 birds were released at three sites on Oahu as of 1979. The best place to see Koloa is at Waimea Falls Park on Oahu, but the birds also have been released on the Kaneohe Marine Corps Air Station and at Kawainui Marsh. Koloa apparently nest throughout the year although the main breeding season on Kauai appears to be from December through May. The eggs are immaculate with a ground color of white, buff, or light tan. The average clutch size is eight eggs and the incubation period is 28 days. Koloa are capable of breeding when one year old. This duck nests on the ground and is subject to predation by mongooses, pigs and dogs. The small, downy young often are eaten by bullfrogs and bass.

Hawaiian Gallinule or 'Alae 'Ula, *Gallinula chloropus sandvicensis.*

This is an endemic subspecies of the Common Gallinule of North America and Eurasia. The Hawaiian birds are nonmigratory, and no one knows when they first reached the Islands. In Hawaiian mythology, the gallinule of Maui felt sorry because the people did not know about fire. The bird flew to the home of the gods, stole a burning branch and returned it to Maui. On the return flight to earth, however, the bird's white forehead became scorched by the flames and was turned red; thus we find that the gallinule has a red forehead (frontal shield) to this day.

The gallinule formerly inhabited most of the Islands but this endangered bird is now believed to be restricted to Kauai and Oahu. Only 194 gallinules were counted on the two islands during the January 1982 census by the State Division of Forestry and Wildlife. The U.S. Fish and Wildlife Service has acquired five refuges for water birds since 1970. A study of the birds at the Hanalei National Wildlife Refuge on Kauai revealed that there was a peak in nesting from April through June but that gallinules probably nest throughout the year in Hawaii. The birds at Hanalei nested in taro patches, where the water was much shallower than is preferred by gallinules on the Mainland. The average clutch size was 5.6 eggs and the incubation period was 22 days. The adults feed the downy chicks until they are about three weeks old.

Hawaiian Coot or 'Alae Ke'oke'O, *Fulica americana alai*.

This is a subspecies of the American Coot that has an extensive breeding range from Canada southward to Panama. The coot also is nonmigratory. Hawaiian Coots are darker in color, have a more slender bill and a larger frontal shield than the North American birds. The frontal shield typically is white, although chocolate-brown shields have been reported. Most of the Hawaiian Coots are now found on Kauai, Oahu and Maui; about 700 birds were counted during January 1982. They are readily seen at Kanaha Pond, Maui. Coots occupy the same general habitat as gallinules but prefer more open water, and often they are seen on brackish water. Their need for deeper water results partly because coots build large floating nests of aquatic vegetation. The nests are anchored frequently to emergent vegetation and rise and fall with changes in water level. The birds apparently nest throughout the year in Hawaii. The newly hatched chicks are covered with black down except on the head, neck and throat, where the down is reddish-orange. The down is short or absent on the forehead and crown, giving the bird a bald-headed appearance; the bill is red to orange-red, tipped with black. Like gallinule chicks, the young coots are able to swim shortly after they hatch and their down has dried.

Hawaiian Stilt or Āeʻo, *Himantopus mexicanus knudseni*.

The Hawaiian Stilt is a subspecies of the Black-necked Stilt of both the East and West coasts of North America and southward to Brazil and the Galapagos Islands. The Hawaiian birds differ from continental birds in having more black on the forehead and the sides of the neck, and by having a longer bill and tail. Fewer than 700 birds were counted by state personnel during January 1982. The largest populations occur on Oahu and Maui. Studies of color-marked birds reveal that stilts fly from one island to another, especially between Niihau and Kauai. Kanaha Pond on Maui and several federal refuges (Pearl Harbor National Wildlife Refuge and the James Campbell refuge near Kahuku on Oahu) are of critical importance for the survival of the stilt and other endangered water birds. The breeding season of the stilt extends from mid-February into August. The nest is a simple scrape made on the ground in sparsely vegetated areas; small stones, bits of wood and other debris often are added to form a partial lining. The normal clutch is four eggs. The eggs are beautifully camouflaged and it is difficult to locate a nest even when the adults give their loud alarm calls nearby. The incubation period varies between 24 and 26 days. The downy young are covered with a coat of variegated brown, buff and black down, which makes them very difficult to find when they leave the nest. The adults do not feed the young but do lead them to suitable feeding areas.

3.
Endemic Land Birds

BUTEO SOLITARIUS

FEWER THAN 15 PERCENT of these unique Hawaiian birds still exist in numbers large enough so that they are not considered to be threatened or endangered. Only in the Mascarene Islands has the birdlife suffered such decimation at the hands of man and the mammals that he has introduced. The most common of these nonendangered land birds are discussed below, as are some of the more remarkable species whose future is uncertain.

Hawaiian Hawk or 'Io, *Buteo solitarius*. (Illustration above.)

This hawk has two color phases. Dark-phase birds have dark brown plumage both above and below. Light-phase birds have dark upperparts and light buff underparts, frequently streaked with darker feathers. As is characteristic of birds of prey, the females are larger than the males. The 'Io occurs only on the island of Hawaii. Classified as an endangered species, with a total population estimate in the low hundreds, the 'Io is widely distributed on Hawaii, being found on both the windward and Kona coasts of Mauna Loa, on the slopes of Mauna Kea and Kohala Mountain. The chief reason for the drastic reduction in numbers of this beneficial species is thought to be illegal shooting by uninformed people who think that all hawks are "chicken hawks." In Hawaii the hawk's primary diet seems to consist of mice, rats, frogs, spiders, insects and their caterpillars; they have been known to have eaten a Barred Dove and a Common Myna. The few nests that have been reported indicate a nesting season lasting from May to October. The eggs have a light blue shell and the clutch is said to consist of two or three eggs. The hawks habitually soar in wide circles at considerable heights above the ground. A soaring bird seen on Hawaii, however, is not necessarily a hawk because the diurnal Hawaiian Owl also soars. Iolani was the sacred hawk in Hawaiian mythology.

Hawaiian Owl or Pueo, *Asio flammeus sandwichensis.*

This endemic subspecies of the Short-eared Owl occurs on all of the main islands, and may be found from sea level to at least 8,000 feet elevation on Maui and Hawaii. The Pueo differs from most other owls in

being diurnal in habit and for its propensity for soaring, often high in the sky. The Pueo also flies low over pastures and fields, sometimes hovering before diving to the ground to catch its prey. This usually consists of mice but also includes Polynesian rats and even the much larger roof rat. The nest is built on the ground and the nearly round eggs are white. Owls begin to incubate after the first egg is laid and, because that egg hatches first, there is a conspicuous difference in size among the nestlings. Although not classified as a threatened species, there appears to have been a noticeable decline in numbers during recent decades. The Pueo played an important role in Hawaiian mythology. Human sacrifices were offered to certain owl gods in the belief that the corpses would be transformed into owls, and such sacrifices also were made to Pele, the goddess of volcanoes. An owl god on Kauai was said to call together all of the other owls on that island and to drive the Menehune from a valley near Pu-u-pueo or owl hill. Owls also served as family protectors, especially in battles. Even in defeat, the flight of an owl might show the vanquished where to hide, "protected by the wings of an owl."

25

Hawaiian Thrush or ʻŌmaʻo, *Phaeornis obscurus.*

The Hawaiian Thrush is primarily a bird of the rain forests where 300 inches of rain may fall in a single year. Here the thrush is at home in the ohia forests where giant tree ferns grow in profusion on the irregular lava substrate that forms the forest floor and where gaping holes and crevices typically are concealed by a luxuriant growth of mosses, vines and smaller ferns. Formerly this thrush inhabited most of the Islands except Maui, but the subspecies on Lanai and Oahu are extinct and only a few birds remain on Molokai; the Kauai race, the Kamao, is classified as an endangered species. Fortunately, the race on Hawaii is common in suitable habitat, usually above 2,500 feet elevation. They can be seen and heard at Volcanoes National Park, along Stainback Highway and along the Saddle Road. Many people feel that the ʻŌmaʻo has the finest song of any endemic species. The males frequently sing while perched on the very top branch of a dead tree, but they also have a flight song in which a bird flies from its lofty perch 50 or more feet above the ground. The bird sings during its gradually arched upward flight, then dives downward to a perch in the forest. The birds also have a low meowlike call and a hoarse alarm note. A peculiar characteristic behavior pattern is its frequent wing quivering, in which the wings are fluttered rapidly while being held below the level of the bird's body. Bulky nests are built in tree ferns or in tree cavities. Two eggs form the clutch.

26

Hawaiian Crow or 'Alalā, *Corvus tropicus.*

The Hawaiian Crow differs from North American crows in being a duller black in color and in having the wings tinged with brown; the feathers of the throat are stiff, with hairlike webs and grayish shafts. The 'Alalā is endemic to the island of Hawaii only. During the 1890s the crow was common from Puuwaawaa southward along the Kona coast and into the Ka'u district as far as Volcanoes National Park. The population now is estimated to number less than 100 birds that occupy only a small part of their former range. The reasons for the great decline in numbers are imperfectly known. George Munro wrote that the Hawaiians used the crow's black feathers for making kahilis, as well as for dressing idols. He also reported that farmers "made war" on the crows in the late 1890s, and shooting is believed to be one of the main reasons for the decline in numbers. The effect of the great alteration in the habitat on the decline is unknown, as are the possible effects of bird diseases, such as malaria and pox. Few nests have been studied but most have been found from April to June; nest success has been low. A captive rearing program was initiated at Pohakuloa during 1976, using young birds that were picked up in the wild, but no young had been raised as of 1982. During 1981, however, Peter Luscomb raised three young that had been hatched from artificially incubated eggs at the Honolulu Zoo.

27

Small Kauai Thrush or Puaiohi, *Phaeornis palmeri*.

The Puaiohi is known to inhabit only the ohia forests of the Alakai Swamp now, where it is believed to be more common than the larger thrush. Because of its very restricted distribution, the Puaiohi is classified as an endangered species, with a total population of less than 100 birds. In addition to being smaller than the Kamao, the Puaiohi has flesh-colored legs (not dark brown), it has a longer and narrower bill, and usually has a distinct white eye-ring. The Puaiohi is primarily a bird of the thickets and understory of the rich rain forest, at times flying to the forest floor. The males, however, often seek high, exposed perches for singing. The first nest of the Puaiohi was discovered by Cameron and Angela Kepler on May 12, 1981. The nest was built in a small cavity about four feet above the ground in a 20-foot-high vertical, vegetated earth bank. The nest cavity was concealed by a heavy growth of an endemic fern, and native shrubs and tree ferns nearby provided shade for the nest and perches for the adult birds. The nest itself was constructed largely of bryophytes and tiny ferns held together with fine grass. The nest held two nearly fully feathered nestlings, with down and sooty-gray pin feathers on the head and neck. The iris was dark brown and the inside of the mouth, bright orange. The Keplers noted that all of the Puaiohi observed were found in deep gorges with flowing water or in smaller, shaded stream beds.

Laysan and Nihoa Millerbirds, *Acrocephalus familiaris*. (Opposite page.)

These are Hawaii's only representatives of the Old World warbler family (Sylviidae). When considering the isolation of the Hawaiian Islands, it is puzzling, indeed, to account for the establishment of such small land birds on Laysan and Nihoa islands. The two populations were isolated long enough to have changed sufficiently in plumage characters and bill length

so that taxonomists recognize them to be races of the same species. They were named "millerbirds" because of their fondness for small moths, called millers. The Laysan Millerbird was first collected by Henry Palmer and George Munro in 1891. For the next 22 years, the millerbird was one of the most common of the four kinds of endemic land birds on the island. About 1903, the manager of the guano mining company on Laysan Island released rabbits on the island. In less than 20 years, the rabbits destroyed nearly all of the vegetation on the island and when Alexander Wetmore, the leader of the Tanager Expedition, reached the island in 1923, the millerbird had become extinct. The Nihoa Millerbird was discovered by Alexander Wetmore in 1923. Nihoa is a mere 156-acre remnant of a once larger island. The Nihoa Millerbird (less than 5.5 inches in length) is a secretive species, spending most of its time in the knee-high cover of goosefoot (*Chenopodium sandwicheum*) and ilima (*Sida fallax*). Nests have held two eggs or young, and the nesting season appears to last from March through August. The birds have a somewhat bubbling and metallic song that does not carry very far, largely because of the pounding surf below and the piercing calls of the thousands of terns on the island.

Oahu 'Elepaio, *Chasiempis sandwichensis gayi.*

This is the only member of the very large (more than 300 species) Old World flycatcher family (Muscicapidae) to reach the Hawaiian Islands. The ancestors are presumed to have come from Melanesia. It is curious that since the discovery of the Islands by Captain Cook, the 'Elepaio has occurred only on Kauai, Oahu and Hawaii. We have no evidence of its presence on Molokai, Lanai, or Maui, three separate islands that at one time were united into a single island. The 'Elepaio was important in Hawaiian mythology. Lea, a goddess, often assumed the form of an 'Elepaio; both goddess and bird were worshipped by canoe builders. In legends involving magical births, heroes, such as Kawelo, might take the form of a man, an 'Elepaio, or other animal. The Oahu 'Elepaio, unlike most endemic land birds, has been able to adapt to manmade changes in the habitat and the birds are readily seen in the introduced forests in Manoa, Moanalua and North Halawa valleys. The nesting season on Oahu lasts from mid-January to mid-June. The small nests are very neat and compact and are held together by spider web. Nests are found at an average of about 25 feet above the ground; the height varies from 8.5 to 50 feet. Both sexes aid in building the nest. The clutch size is usually two eggs, and the long incubation period is 18 days. The name 'Elepaio comes from one of the variations in the bird's primary song. Both sexes sing, and singing is especially pronounced during the courtship and nest-building stages. Singing is infrequent during the incubation period, but increases after the young hatch, increasing again after they leave the nest.

Kauai 'Ō'Ō, *Moho braccatus.*

This very rare bird is the only one of five Hawaiian members of the Old World honeyeater family (Meliphagidae) that is not extinct. The 'Ō'Ō of Oahu, Molokai and Hawaii have been extinct since early this century and the Kioea of Hawaii has not been seen since about 1859. The Kauai 'Ō'Ō was the smallest of the four species, its total length ranging between 7.5 and 8.5 inches; by contrast the male Hawaii 'Ō'Ō was between 12 and 13 inches long. Honeyeaters, as their name suggests, are primarily nectar-feeders, and the tongue is highly specialized for obtaining the nectar from flowers. The extinct species of 'Ō'Ō had patches of bright yellow feathers, which were highly prized by the Hawaiians in their feather work. N. B. Emerson wrote that the "plumage birds, like everything else in Hawaii, were the property of the *alii* of the land, and as such were protected by *tabu*; at least that was the case in the reign of Kamehameha I and for some time before. The choicest of the feathers found their way into the possession of the kings and chiefs, being largely used in payment of annual tribute." The Kauai 'Ō'Ō was said to be numerous in many places and widely distributed during the 1890s. Now there may be no more than a dozen birds in the forests of the Alakai Swamp, where more than 600 inches (50 feet!) of rain have been recorded in a single year. The reasons for the decline in population are unknown. John L. Sincock discovered the first nest of the Kauai 'Ō'Ō on May 31, 1971, and others the following two years. The nests were built in tree cavities 25 to 40 feet from the ground; all of the nests held two young birds.

Palila, *Loxoides bailleui.*

Many of the forest birds have only a Hawaiian name and the Latin scientific name. Such is the case for this finch-billed member of the endemic Hawaiian honeycreeper family (Drepanididae). The life of the Palila is inextricably tied to the mamane-naio forest on the slopes of Mauna Kea above elevations of about 6,000 feet, and the birds now occupy only about 10 percent of their former range. During much of the year the birds eat the seed pods of the mamane and its flowers, and most nests are built in this tree. Two eggs form a clutch. The Palila shares a trait with cardueline finches: The adults do not remove all of the fecal sacs after the first few days of nestling life, so they accumulate on the nest. The dry mamane-naio forest on Mauna Kea has been subjected to grazing and browsing by horses, cattle, sheep and goats since early in the last century. Introduced feral sheep and mouflon sheep have been responsible for decimating this forest for many years. In 1981 the U.S. 9th Circuit Court of Appeals upheld a federal judge's 1979 ruling that the feral sheep would have to be eliminated from the mountain because they were incompatible with the survival of the forest. In order to insure the future for the Palila, it now will be necessary to eliminate the 500-odd mouflon sheep that still live on Mauna Kea.

Maui Parrotbill, *Pseudonestor xanthophrys.* (Opposite.)

This small (5.5 inches long), olive-green honeycreeper has a short tail and a very large, hooked, parrotlike bill. As its name suggests, it occurs only on the island of Maui, where it is restricted to the outer, windward slope of Haleakala Crater. The species was discovered by Henry Palmer in 1892. It was first reported this century in 1950 and again in 1967. It is one of the rarer honeycreepers in the Maui forests, from Kipahulu Valley to the Hosmer Grove region at elevations between about 5,000 feet and tree line. It undoubtedly occurred at lower elevations before the introduction of mosquitoes (about 1826) to the Islands and before the early Polynesians burned much of the lowland dry forest. R. C. L. Perkins described the foraging activities of the parrotbill in the 1890s, and Stephen R. Sabo studied the birds during 1980 and 1981. Sabo found that the birds prefer areas with an understory consisting of a variety of plants. Most often the birds dig into dead branches of living plants. They insert the hooked upper mandible into a crack or borer hole in the bark and then grasp the bark with both mandibles to peel off pieces of bark and wood. The upper mandible may be used to scrape out old wood or to peck the bark as woodpeckers do. Grubs and pupae are extracted with the tongue. Parrotbills often forage with loose flocks of Maui Creepers. The nests and eggs have not been described.

'Amakihi, *Hemignathus virens.*

The 'Amakihi is a characteristic bird of the wet ohia forests on all of the Islands, although it now is uncommon on Lanai, Molokai and Oahu. Writers of the 1890s found this species common in all native forests above 1,000 feet elevation. It is now unusual to find the 'Amakihi at such low elevations. The birds also inhabit the dry mamane-naio forest on Mauna Kea up to tree line. There it feeds on insects and nectar from the bright yellow mamane flowers; in ohia forests it feeds among the bright red flowers of those trees. Most singing is done from a perch, but the 'Amakihi also has a flight song. The birds are adapted to wide temperature fluctuations at elevations between 6,000 and 9,000 feet on Mauna Kea. During one four-year period, the maximum recorded temperature was 88° F and the minimum was 20°. The temperature did not fall below 37° in only one month of that period. On Mauna

Kea the breeding season sometimes begins by mid-October and continues throughout the winter and spring. On Kauai the birds appear not to initiate the breeding season until February. Both male and female take part in building the nest, in most habitats in ohia trees. The clutch varies from two to four eggs, and the female begins to incubate after she has laid the last egg. She does not sing or call from the nest. When disturbed, she flies off rapidly and quietly without giving any alarm notes. The blind and nearly naked newly hatched young weigh about 1.0 gram. They may weigh as much as 17 grams when 16 days old. The nestling period varies from 17 to 20 days, a long period for passerine birds.

'Anianiau, *Hemignathus parvus.*

    'Anianiau is a mite of a bird, rarely exceeding 4.25 inches in length from tip of bill to tip of tail. It is found only on Kauai, where its range is much reduced from that in the 1890s. It is common now only in the ohia forests that extend from Kokee State Park into the Alakai Swamp. All of the native birds of Kauai are adapted to an environment of cold and rain. Most of the suitable habitat lies at elevations above 3,500 feet, where nighttime temperatures of 39° F or lower are common. During the nonbreeding season, the 'Anianiau can be identified by their simple, sweet "ps-seet" call note as they flit rapidly about in search of food. They feed not only in the crowns of the trees but also in understory plants, including the flowers of the introduced passion fruit (*Passiflora*). The 'Anianiau builds its nest in ohia trees, either in terminal clusters or within very thick clumps of small branches that grow from the main trunk, so that most are very difficult to locate. the usual clutch is two or three eggs, sometimes four. Only the female incubates, and the eggs hatch after 14 days of incubation. The male apparently does not feed the female on the nest, but he frequently feeds her after she leaves the nest. The female then solicits food in a manner similar to that used by nestling birds: She crouches, flutters her wings and gives soft call notes. The nestling period at most nests is 18 days. An 'Anianiau raised in captivity lived to be 9.5 years old.

Nukupuʻu, *Hemignathus lucidus.*

The strongly decurved bill of this species is unique among birds in that the lower mandible is only about half as long as the upper mandible. The three subspecies were found on Kauai, Oahu and Maui. During the 1830s, birds were collected in Nuuanu Valley "at no great elevation above the sea," but the Oahu Nukupuʻu was extinct before 1890. In writing about feral cattle, R. C. L. Perkins wrote in 1903 that "this fine valley is now practically denuded of its forest and largely filled with unsightly guava scrub; and the cliffs on either side, which to Bloxam appeared bare in comparison with the valley itself, now alone retain their native vegetation. Of late years, some attempt has been made to reforest the head of the valley, but the exotic trees now planted are a poor substitute for the many rare and beautiful native species, which once flourished there; nor is it likely that any reforesting will bring back the birds which the American and Prussian naturalists found so plentiful some sixty-five years ago." He was correct, of course. The Kauai Nukupuʻu is restricted to the depths of the Alakai Swamp; the Maui birds are found only in the rain forests on the windward slopes of Haleakala Crater. Both exist in low numbers and truly are endangered species.

'Akiapola'au, *Hemignathus wilsoni.*

In this species the upper mandible is strongly decurved whereas the lower mandible is straight, robust and only about half as long as the slender and more delicate upper mandible. Despite its unique bill, it is not always easy to distinguish the 'Akiapola'au from the Hawaii 'Amakihi in the field. Male Hawaii 'Amakihi often have a similar bright yellow plumage and the size difference is not obvious when the two species are flitting rapidly in the dense foliage. During the 1890s the 'Akiapola'au was widely distributed on the island of Hawaii, to which island it is confined. It is now much restricted in distribution, being found in the mamane-naio forest above 6,000 feet on Mauna Kea, in some ohia forests on the windward slopes of Mauna Kea and Mauna Loa, and in two widely separated areas on the Kona coast. The feeding habits of the 'Akiapola'au sometimes resemble those of the Brown Creeper (*Certhia familiaris*): The birds begin at the bottom of a tree and work upward in a spiral path along the trunk. The birds also have woodpeckerlike feeding habits, pounding the lower mandible into dead branches and tree trunks in their search for insects and their grubs. The nesting season lasts at least from October to May, thus indicating that the breeding season for the 'Akiapola'au begins when the days are growing shorter.

Kauai 'Ākepa, *Loxops coccineus*. (Left.)

The 'Ākepa is noted because of its short conical bill in which the horny, covering layers of the upper and lower mandibles are twisted in opposite directions, hence the genus name *Loxops*, meaning "twisted face." Perkins wrote that these "are among the most active native birds and their name 'Ākepa, signifying 'sprightly,' 'turning this way and that,' is singularly appropriate." Other subspecies evolved on Oahu, Maui and Hawaii; the males on Maui vary from brownish-orange to dull yellow and the Hawaii males are red-orange to ruby colored. All are small birds four to five inches in length. The Oahu race is extinct; those on Maui and Hawaii are classified as endangered birds. The Kauai 'Ākepa can be seen in the ohia forests at Kokee State Park. Like the 'Amakihi, the 'Ākepa seek their food primarily from the leaves and twigs rather than from the trunks and larger branches. Perkins found during the 1890s that the 'Ākepa feeds largely on caterpillars and spiders, occasionally drinking the nectar from ohia and other flowers. He felt confident that this species was "of high value in the forests," destroying quantities of insects which "are well concealed and obtained only to a comparatively small extent or not at all, by the other native birds." C. Robert Eddinger discovered the first nest of the Kauai 'Ākepa on March 9, 1969. This nest was being built by both sexes about 30 feet from the ground in an ohia tree. Unfortunately, this nest was deserted after one egg had been laid. The first nest of the Hawaii 'Ākepa was found by John L. Sincock on May 12, 1976, when he flushed a female from a cavity only three feet from the ground in an ohia tree. There were three eggs in the nest.

'I'Iwi, *Vestiaria coccinea*. (Opposite.)

This species has the most striking plumage of the common honeycreepers and its long, decurved, salmon-colored bill also is distinctive. Immature birds are greenish-yellow to brownish-yellow, and they present many color combinations as the red feathers of the adult begin to grow in among the juvenile feathers. The 'I'Iwi formerly inhabited all of the main islands but now is extinct on Lanai and is rare on Molokai and Oahu. It is, however, common in the rain forests on Hawaii, Maui and Kauai. The red blossoms of the ohia tree appear now to be the most important source of nectar for this species, but it also feeds from a wide variety of flowers, including the yellow flowers of the mamane and a number of introduced species. Titian Peale wrote after the United States Exploring Expedition of 1838 to 1842 that on Oahu he found 'I'Iwi "generally about the gigantic lobelias which characterize the botany of that interesting island; they extract their food from the flowers of the lobelia, for which their singularly-formed bill is admirably adapted." The birds also eat many kinds of insects. 'I'Iwi nests are built primarily of twigs and are lined with lichens and mosses. The females lay two or three eggs in a clutch. The incubation period is 14 days. When they hatch, the young have orange-pink skin and the bill is short and straight. By the end of

the nestling stage (21 or 22 days), the bill is obviously elongated and slightly decurved and is a light horn-color. When they leave the nest, the young birds are able to fly with ease from tree to tree.

Crested Honeycreeper or ʻĀkohekohe, _Palmeria dolei._

This remarkably plumaged bird once inhabited the ohia forests of Molokai and Maui. It is extinct on Molokai and little is known about the biology of the Maui population. It now is known that the species is relatively common in a restricted habitat on the outer slopes of Haleakala Crater, extending from Manawainui and Kipahulu valleys northwestward to the forests just west of the Koolau Gap, and at elevations between 4,200 and 7,100 feet. Perkins noted that the "diet of nectar appears to be obtained almost entirely if not solely from the flowers of the Ohia, and the whitish frontal crest is sometimes filled with the entangled pollen grains from these blossoms. It is also partial to caterpillars, and not only obtains those which feed upon the foliage but also searches the dead branches of trees in dense wet woods for those which feed on this substance." Perkins also noted that "its call note is a simple clear whistle, very easily imitated, and by this means the bird can always be easily called in numbers in a good locality." On one occasion, Perkins "assembled no less than nine adult birds at the same time in one small Ohia tree not more than twenty feet high." The nest and eggs have not been described, but immature birds have been seen during early May.

'Apapane, *Himatione sanguinea.*

This is the most common of the surviving species of honeycreeper, and one subspecies occupies all of the main islands. A second race evolved on Laysan Island, but that population became extinct in 1923. In contrast to the deep crimson color of the adults, immature birds are grayish-brown above and buff-colored below. All kinds of intermediate plumages are seen during the period that the young birds are acquiring their adult plumage. The 'Apapane is typically found in the crown of the forest, whether the trees are 25 or 100 feet high. They are gregarious during much of the year, and are conspicuous both because of their numbers and because of their chorus of calls as they fly from one tree to another to feed among the ohia blossoms. Their wings produce a distinctive whirring noise in flight that is audible for some distance. This phenomenon also is found in the 'I'Iwi and Crested Honeycreeper. The 'Apapane makes longer and higher flights than the other species of honeycreeper. One researcher taped 'Apapane songs in different habitats on several islands and found so many different songs that he wrote, "we decided that the musicianship of the 'Apapane appears to be unsurpassed." Nests usually are placed in ohia trees, sometimes at considerable heights above the ground. They also build nests on the upper surface of drooping tree fern fronds, and still other nests have been found in lava tubes on Mauna Loa.

4. The Introduced Birds

LIKE ALL OF THE IMMIGRANT races of man that now call Hawaii their home, the introduced birds are now birds of Hawaii, even though their original home was Asia, Africa or South America.

Many of the introduced species live in the lowlands or in upland areas where most of the native vegetation was destroyed many years ago. The vast majority of birds seen by tourists are these exotic species. Several species, however, have invaded the rain forests where most of the endemic forest birds live. Among these invaders are the Melodious Laughing Thrush, Red-billed Leiothrix and the Japanese White-eye. It has not yet been shown to what extent they compete with, and are a hazard to, the native species, especially the honeycreepers.

The apparent advantages of introducing exotic birds to an island habitat with a scarcity of native birds are obvious: We need more songsters; we need more game birds; we need more birds to destroy the insect (or weed) pests that reduce our cattle and agricultural profits. However, problems often result that are not anticipated by those who proclaim such simple and "meritorious" reasons for introductions. Although it does eat army worms and other pests, the Common Myna also eats lantana berries and then spreads this noxious weed, as do the exotic doves. Seed-eating birds also eat rice and other small-grain crops. Some introduced birds have harbored parasites and other diseases, and every new study has revealed worm parasites not previously recorded in the Islands. Even an introduced species that does not survive may pass its parasites along to other established species. The endemic forest birds appear to be highly susceptible to bird malaria, a common bird blood disease in some introduced birds in Hawaii. More than 25 different diseases can be transmitted from birds to man, so the diseases and parasites of exotic species may affect the endemic forest birds, game birds, commercial poultry or man.

Cattle Egret, *Bubulcus ibis*. (Opposite.)

This is an Old World bird, native to southern Eurasia and northern Africa. Cattle Egrets reached the New World unaided by man, being first recorded in British Guiana in 1930. By 1962 the birds were nesting in southern Canada and by 1965 the birds had reached California. Cattle Egrets were imported to Hawaii in 1959 to aid "in the battle to control house flies, horn flies, and other flies that damage hides and cause lower weight gains in cattle." A total of 105 birds was released on five islands during July and August 1959. By 1962 the population on Oahu exceeded 150 birds; now, several thousand Cattle Egrets are found on Oahu, the largest concentrations being at roosts on the Kaneohe Marine Corps Air Station and at Pearl Harbor. Some 25 birds were released on Kauai during 1959, and no more than that number were counted up until 1975 on the semiannual water bird censuses conducted by personnel of the State Division of Forestry and Wildlife; during 1980, however, the Kauai population was estimated to be at least 6,800 birds. Cattle Egrets habitually feed with cattle, horses and water buffalo, as well as with wild grazing animals in other parts of the world. They feed close to the mouths of the animals and often perch on their backs, eating the insects

on the animals and those disturbed by their movements. The
egrets also feed where cattle are absent: for example, in
plowed sugar cane and pineapple fields, newly cut alfalfa
fields, along highways and even on lawns in residential areas.

California quail,
*Lophortyx
californicus.*

Two geographical races of this quail were introduced to the Hawaiian Islands prior to 1855: California Coast Quail and California Valley Quail. They are now common on all the islands except Lanai and Oahu. In their 1949 study of the game birds in Hawaii, Charles and Elizabeth Schwartz remarked that the distribution of the two subspecies of the California Quail in the Hawaiian Islands "presents a puzzling picture because here the climatic conditions do not appear to conform to the general pattern of their original California distribution." They believed that "the survival of these particular races was determined by elements of chance at the time of their introduction accompanied by subsequently favorable land use rather than by adaptations to particular environmental factors." On Hawaii the birds occur up to tree line on the slopes of Mauna Kea and Mauna Loa. Very large flocks form during the nonbreeding season in the open, parkland-type of mamane-naio forest on Mauna Kea. This quail usually roosts in thickly foliaged trees at night, and it often rests by perching in trees during the daytime. The nesting season begins in February and extends to late July. The eggs are laid in a slight depression on the ground after the hen has scratched away whatever cover was present; she may then add dried grasses and leaves as a scanty lining to the depression. The hen lays from six to 12 creamy white eggs covered with spots and blotches of golden brown. As a rule, only the hen incubates the eggs, which hatch after 22 or 23 days. The eggs and the flightless chicks are especially vulnerable to mongooses, rats and feral cats.

Indian Chukar Partridge, *Alectoris chukar*. (Opposite.)

This large partridge is native to the Himalaya Mountains of India and Nepal. Taxonomists recognize some 22 different geographical races of the Chukar; these have a wide distribution that extends from Italy, Sicily and Palestine east to Mongolia, northern China and Manchuria, and south to the Himalayas. Male Chukars are pugnacious and Chukar fighting is a popular sport in northeastern Pakistan and India.

The Indian Chukar inhabits stony mountainsides with a sparse growth of scrub vegetation, rocky ravines and river valleys in which terraced agriculture is practiced. In such country the birds range from about 4,000 to 16,000 feet elevation. Indian Chukars apparently were first imported by the City and County of Honolulu in 1923 and liberated on Oahu; 17 birds were released on Hawaii in 1949; by 1955 the estimated population on Hawaii was 30,000 birds. Turkish Chukars also were imported by the State Division of Fish and Game during the period of 1959 to 1961 and released on all islands except Hawaii. The Chukar is most common on Hawaii (especially on Mauna Kea and Hualalai) and on Maui (in Haleakala Crater). Chukars also occur at the Kuaokala Game Management Area in the Kaena Point region of Oahu. The simplest nest is merely a scrape on the ground under a bush or overhanging rock. Some hens line the scrape with grasses, leaves and rootlets. The clutch seems to vary from seven to 12 eggs. The background color of the eggshell varies from yellowish to grayish; reddish spots are scattered over much of the surface of the shell. Chukars have 14 different calls that are related to social contact, sexual behavior and alarm situations.

Indian Gray and Indian Black Francolins, *Francolinus pondicerianus interpositus* and *F. f. asiae.*

These two species of francolin are native to northern India. The Gray Francolin is a bird of dry grasslands, tropical thorn-scrub country and subtropical dry forests at elevations up to 1,500 feet. It often is found near Indian villages and cultivated land. The birds typically run very fast along the ground when disturbed. As is true for most game birds, the birds' wings make a very startling sound when the birds do flush and swiftly take to wing. This francolin also is kept as a fighting bird. In India, the Black Francolin prefers areas near rivers, streams and canals, where the birds spend much of their time in dense cover. They also like areas where they can forage for food in cultivated lands, especially grain and sugar cane fields. The birds are omnivorous, eating a wide variety of cereal grains, seeds of grasses and weeds, leaves, fruits, berries, and both adult and larval insects. Both species have an extended breeding season in India, lasting from March to September or October. Some 1,700 Gray Francolin and 750 Black Francolin were imported by the State Division of Fish and Game between 1959 and 1962. An additional 116 Black Francolin were imported by the owners of the Puuwaawaa Ranch during the same period. On Hawaii the Gray Francolin now occurs from sea level on the leeward coast to about 7,500 feet in the mamane-naio forest on Mauna Kea; the Black Francolin is common at lower elevations, especially the kiawe thickets from Mahukona to Puako. Both species are found on Kauai, Molokai and Maui, and the Gray Francolin, on Lanai.

Erckel's Francolin, *Francolinus e. erckelii.* (Opposite.)

This very large francolin is native to the entire Ethiopian highland; a second subspecies is found in the Red Sea province of the Egyptian Sudan. Very little seems to be known about either the details of ecological distribution or habits of this species in its native habitat. Almost 1,400 Erckel's Francolin were imported by the State Division of Fish and Game and the owners of the Puuwaawaa Ranch on Hawaii from 1957 to 1962. These were released on all islands except Niihau. As of 1969, the species apparently had failed to become established on Maui and Molokai; it was established locally on Kauai, Oahu and Hawaii, and had occupied habitats some distance from the release site on Lanai. There is a limited amount of habitat for Erckel's Francolin on Oahu, but a population maintains itself in the west end of the Waianae Mountains, where the birds inhabit the mixed native and introduced forest consisting of such plants as guava, haole koa, silk oak, wiliwili and sandalwood. This francolin continues to

become a more important game bird on Kauai. There the birds seem to prefer areas where the dominant vegetation is composed of koa, silk, oak and pukiawe. Erckel's Francolin now has a wide distribution on Lanai and Hawaii. The release sites on Hawaii represented three different ecosystems at different elevations. From the Puako release site at sea level, the birds have spread out through the dry mesquite areas north of Kawaihae. In the Pohakuloa region (elevation 6,500 feet), the birds inhabit the mamane-naio forest.

Japanese Quail, *Coturnix c. japonica.*

This small quail (about 8 inches in total length) is native to Korea, Manchuria, southeastern China and the islands of Japan. The eight subspecies, however, have a very extensive range that includes the Azores, Madeira, Canary and Cape Verde islands, Africa, Europe and eastward to Asia and India. This bird is known as the Eastern Quail in parts of China, the Japanese Gray Quail in India and simply the Quail in Japan. There are four different species in the genus *Coturnix* and these are the only truly migratory species in the entire order of gallinaceous birds (the Galliformes). *Coturnix coturnix* also is called the migratory quail: It is this species that is referred to in the Bible (Exodus 16:13 *et seq.*). One student of the subject estimated that the Children of Israel killed more than eight million quail during a two-day period. Several million quail were killed annually in Egypt and the Middle East during the early part of the present century. This quail has long been kept as a cage bird in Japan, primarily because of its pleasant call notes. During the present century, they also have been kept for meat and eggs. By raising the birds under continuous artificial light, the hens begin to lay when less than two months of age and they may lay as many as 300 eggs per year. Japanese Quail were first imported to Hawaii in 1921; these birds were released on Maui and Lanai. At a later date, the birds presumably were introduced to the other islands. They now appear to be uncommon on Oahu, and the highest densities are thought to be on Hawaii and Maui. In Hawaii the males begin their territorial and courtship calls during February, and the nesting season lasts from March through September (no intensive studies have been conducted). During the breeding season, the males may call every 10 to 15 seconds in the early morning hours.

White-crested Kaleej Pheasant, *Lophura leucomelana.* (Opposite.)

This large pheasant is native to the Himalayan foothills from the Indus River in India eastward into Nepal, and from southern China southward to Burma and western Thailand. In its native habitat, this pheasant is found in both deciduous and evergreen forests that have a dense understory, and it is found in bamboo thickets and dense shrub-grown areas. In Nepal, the birds show a preference for dense vegetation near streams and terraced agriculture, but, during the summer months, some birds move upward in the mountains to elevations

exceeding 11,000 feet. The cocks are pugnacious during the breeding season; their primary call has been described as a "loud whistling chuckle." By rapidly vibrating his wings against the body, the cock also produces a drumming sound "like cloth fluttering in the breeze." The hen builds a nest of grasses, leaves and other plant materials in a shallow depression in the ground. The eggs are unmarked and have a ground color that varies from whitish to buff. Victor Lewin reported that 67 Kaleej Pheasants were released on the Puuwaawaa Ranch in 1962. He described these birds as being "shy forest dwellers" that were never seen in the vicinity of any of the sanctuaries for game birds that had been constructed on the ranch property. Since that time, however, the Kaleej Pheasants have been very successful and now occur not only on the Kona coast (for example, Kahaluu Forest Reserve, Kaloko Mauka subdivision) but also on the windward face of Mauna Kea and Mauna Loa (Keauhou Ranch, and ohia forests along Stainback Highway).

Indian Peafowl, *Pavo cristatus.*

The peafowl is found throughout India and Ceylon. The peacock was selected as the national bird of India in 1963. A second species, the Green Peafowl, is found in Burma, Thailand and southward through the Malay Peninsula to Java. In India the birds are found from sea level to about 6,000 feet elevation in the foothills of the Himalayas. They are omnivorous, eating grain, seeds, berries, flower buds, centipedes, scorpions, worms, lizards, small snakes and a wide variety of insects. The peacock is polygamous: Each cock has from three to five hens. The cock has an elaborate courtship display or "dance," in which he raises and fans his train. Periodically, the cock shakes so violently that the quills of the train produce a distinct "zizzing" sound, after which the cock pivots and displays his black rump and the undersurface of the train to the hen. The spectacular train of the peacock is not composed of the tail feathers themselves but of highly specialized upper tail coverts. Peacocks roost at night in trees and when going to roost in the evening and before leaving it in the morning, the birds give loud raucous calls, readily heard from the Proud Peacock restaurant at Waimea Falls Park. The nest typically is built on the ground, but at the park, the hens sometimes nest in the crotch of a large tree. Peafowl were first brought to Hawaii in 1860 and now are found on all of the islands except Lanai.

Spotted Dove, *Streptopelia chinensis.* (Opposite.)

This dove was first given a scientific name in 1786 from specimens collected in China. The species has a much wider range, however, extending from Ceylon and India through Burma and the Malay Peninsula to Borneo, Sumatra and Java. Other names for this dove are Lace-necked Dove, Necklace Dove and Chinese Turtle Dove. In addition to Hawaii, this dove has been introduced to California, Mauritius and parts of Australia. The date of introduction to Hawaii is unknown. The birds were kept as cage birds by the Chinese, who also raised them for food. The Spotted Dove was reported to be common on Oahu as early as 1879. They now are abundant on all islands, being most common from sea level to about 4,000 feet elevation, although they do occur in smaller numbers to 8,000 feet. They occur in regions with as little as 10 inches of annual rainfall and those with over 100 inches. Doves are noted for building frail platforms of twigs as nests; often the eggs can be seen through the bottom of the nest. Nests are made in a variety ot places, from a few inches off the ground to 20 or more feet

above it. The eggs are glossy white, and the female almost invariably lays two eggs per clutch. The nestlings are fed "pigeon's milk," a protein-rich secretion from the adult bird's crop. The birds may breed throughout the year in Hawaii, but most nesting is said to take place between February and November. The male has a display flight during which he flies upward in an arching curve from the top of a tree and then glides down again with wings and tail outspread to land in another tree. The Spotted Dove in Hawaii is considered to be "one of the favored 'easy hunting' game birds."

Susan G. Monden

Barred Dove, *Geopelia striata*.

The native range of this dove includes the Philippine Islands, Malaysia and southward to New Guinea and Australia. It also has been introduced to Thailand, St. Helena and Madagascar. It is a common cage bird throughout Malaysia. It is called the Zebra Dove in most of its native range, but Barred Dove in Borneo. Edward L. Caum referred to it as the Bar-shouldered Dove in his paper on the introduced birds of Hawaii. According to Caum, this dove was "imported from Australia in 1922 by the City and County of Honolulu for liberation on Oahu, and by Mrs. D. R. Isenberg for liberation on Kauai." Charles and Elizabeth Schwartz reported densities as high as 800 birds per square mile in certain habitats on Molokai and Oahu in 1947. At that time, the Barred Dove occurred from sea level to about 3,000 feet elevation. This very successful immigrant now can be found at elevations of 6,500 feet and higher. The highest densities are found where the introduced kiawe and haole koa flourish. Feeding stations supplied with mixed bird seed attract large numbers of Barred Doves, even in downtown Honolulu, and the birds also are conspicuous in Waikiki, where they walk about amid diners at outdoor restaurants. The diet of the Barred Dove consists of about 97 percent seeds and other plant materials and about three percent animal matter, including weevils, beetles and wireworm larvae. It is from their insect food that the doves become infected with tapeworms and roundworms. Barred Doves probably nest throughout the year in Hawaii. The flimsy nest platform, made primarily of twigs, is placed from a few feet to more than 20 feet above the ground. The females lay two white eggs.

Barn Owl, *Tyto alba pratincola.*

Barn Owls differ from other owls in that they have a heart-shaped facial disc of feathers; hence the name monkey-faced owls. Eleven different species of Barn Owls are distributed throughout most of the world; they are absent as native birds only from New Zealand and some oceanic islands. Barn Owls were first released in Hawaii during 1958, and from April 1959 through June 1963, 71 additional owls were released on Kauai, Oahu, Molokai and Hawaii. These birds were introduced in the hope that they would prey upon the rats that cause so much damage to sugar cane. Mainland Barn Owls are highly beneficial, subsisting largely on mice and rats, but they also eat shrews, ground squirrels, bats, frogs, insects and crayfish. On the island of Hawaii, however, Dr. P. Quentin Tomich analyzed 104 regurgitated owl pellets and found that 91 pellets contained only the remains of the house mouse. He commented that although the Barn Owl in Hawaii does sometimes eat rats, the owl is not likely to be a significant factor in their economic control. Moreover, G. Vernon Byrd and Thomas C. Telfer reported in 1980 that Barn Owls on Kauai and Kaula Island had killed more than 100 sea birds. Further studies are needed to determine just how beneficial the Barn Owl is in Hawaii. Barn Owls are largely nocturnal, whereas the endemic Pueo is largely diurnal in habits. Barn Owls have black eyes; the Pueo, yellow eyes.

Skylark, *Alauda arvensis*. (Lower right, above.)

This is the skylark of English literature. The species has a wide distribution throughout the British Isles, Europe, Asia, Northern Africa and Japan. It has been introduced on Vancouver Island, British Columbia, New Zealand and Hawaii. Edward L. Caum wrote in 1933: "In 1870 Mrs. Frances Sinclair liberated skylarks on Kauai, and in the same year Hon. A. S. Cleghorn imported some from New Zealand and freed them on the high table-land at Leilehua, Oahu....Later, birds were taken from Oahu to Kauai, Maui, Molokai, Lanai, and Hawaii." The largest concentrations now occur on Hawaii, Maui and Lanai; the population on Kauai apparently has died out and the birds are now rare on Oahu. On Hawaii skylarks are found in the pasture lands at South Point and as high as Halepohaku (elevation 9,200 feet) on Mauna Kea. The species also is common on the outer grassy slopes of Haleakala Crater, Maui, as well as in the eastern end of the crater itself. Male skylarks are in full song by the first week of November on Hawaii. From the ground, the males take off to fly high in the air and hover there or fly in circles, singing continuously for several minutes. At the end of the song period, the bird closes its wings and dives swiftly toward the ground. Some skylarks include the notes of other birds in their song, and I have heard several skylarks that included calls of the 'Elepaio in their flight songs. Skylarks build their nests on the ground; we know little about the nesting season in Hawaii. Nests that I have found contained only two eggs, in contrast to a clutch of three to five eggs in England.

Western Meadowlark, *Sturnella neglecta*. (Lower left and upper right, opposite.)

Meadowlarks are members of the family Icteridae, which also includes blackbirds, troupials, New World orioles and the Bobolink. The Western Meadowlark is found as a breeding species from British Columbia, Ontario and Michigan southward into Mexico. In writing about this species in Hawaii, Caum said: "It is a bird of great esthetic and economic value. The species was imported from California in 1931 by the Board of Agriculture and Forestry for liberation on Oahu, and by Mrs. Dora Isenberg for liberation on Kauai." Nothing seems to have been written about the Oahu birds after 1933, but the species did not survive. On Kauai the birds are fairly common but highly localized, being found near Kekaha, Lihue, Kapaa and Kilauea. Nothing seems to have been published about the behavior or nesting habits of the birds in Hawaii. Meadowlarks are primarily ground-inhabiting birds, found in open fields, prairies, pastures and alfalfa fields. The birds walk on the ground, rather than hop. Males, especially, sometimes perch on a weed, fence post or telephone wire, and they sing from such perches; they also sing in flight. Meadowlarks build their domed nests on the ground and these are typically very difficult to locate. The ground color of the eggs is white, greenish-white, or pinkish, covered with spots, speckles and blotches varying in color from brown to lavender. Their diet includes more than 60 percent animal matter, such as wireworms, cutworms, caterpillars, crickets, grasshoppers and ground beetles.

Melodious Laughing Thrush, *Garrulax canorus*.

Although long called the Chinese Thrush in Hawaii, this bird is not a thrush at all but a member of the large babbler family (Timaliidae), an Old World family. The Chinese name is Hwa-mei. The species is native to the Yangtze Valley, China, and southward into northern Laos, and it occurs on Formosa. Harry and John Caldwell wrote in their *South China Birds* that the Hwa-mei was prized as a cage bird because of "its power of song and prowess in battle." Adult males are trapped by placing a trained bird in one compartment of a trap in the territory of a wild male; the wild bird readily enters the trap in response to the singing of the intruder. There is no record of the date of importation of this Laughing Thrush to Hawaii during the last century. Caum wrote in 1933 that this was a favorite cage bird of the Chinese in Hawaii and that a number of birds escaped at the time of "the great fire in the Oriental quarter of Honolulu in 1900." After that date, birds were imported from China and released on Molokai, Maui and Hawaii. In 1918, birds were taken to Kauai. The birds are now found on all of the islands except Lanai. The nesting season in Hawaii lasts from March through July. The three to four eggs in a clutch have an immaculate bluish-green color. The bulky nests are built on the ground and in shrubs and trees, usually under 15 feet from the ground. Laughing Thrushes are typically shy and wary birds. They are more often heard than seen. Their loud, multi-phrased songs consist of musical whistles, churring and chucking sounds, and some buzzy phrases.

White-crested Laughing Thrush, *Garrulax leucolophus.*

This babbler is native to India, the Himalayas and Burma. Like most babblers, this is a noisy, gregarious species, with flocks sometimes numbering 40 individuals in India. They are described as being "very boisterous when disturbed, exploding into choruses of loud cackling 'laughter.'" Their food consists of berries, seeds, insects, small reptiles and flower nectar. In India the nesting season lasts from March to September. The nests are large, shallow cups constructed loosely of grasses, leaves, roots and moss. The usual clutch is four eggs that are immaculate white in color but have tiny pits over the entire surface of the shell. Both sexes incubate the eggs. Two species of parasitic Indian cuckoos often lay their eggs in the nests of this Laughing Thrush. There are no records of the introduction of this species to Hawaii but a pair was reported to be nesting on the slopes of Diamond Head in 1969. Birds also have been seen at Foster Botanical Garden and at Hickam Air Force Base.

Red-whiskered and Red-vented Bulbuls, *Pycnonotus jocosus* and *P. cafer*.

All members of the bulbul family (Pycnonotidae) are "prohibited entry" into Hawaii, but these two species are now very well established. Both species are native to India and the Indo-Chinese region. In March 1977, the U.S. Fish and Wildlife Service proposed that bulbuls be added to the list of "injurious species" that should not be imported into the United States without a special permit (the Red-vented Bulbul has been introduced to the Fiji Islands, where it is considered a serious pest on fruit trees and vegetable gardens); other prohibited species, already found in Hawaii, were the Japanese White-eye, Common Indian Myna and the Java Sparrow. Two Red-whiskered Bulbuls were reported in lower Makiki Heights in 1965; by the fall of 1967, 24 birds were counted in that area. By 1979 the birds were found from Hawaii Kai to Pearl City Heights. The first Red-vented Bulbuls were reported at the Oahu Plantation at Waipahu in 1966. This abundant species now is found from Hanauma Bay to Waipahu and Wahiawa on the Leeward side of Oahu and from Waimanalo to Kuilima on the Windward coast. It will be found throughout the island in only a few years. Bulbuls eat fruits, berries, figs, flower buds, nectar, insects and spiders. The breeding season of the Red-whiskered Bulbul lasts from January into August; that of the Red-vented Bulbul from January into October. Both species of bulbuls are noted for perching in the open on telephone wires or on the topmost branches of trees. Both species flock during the nonbreeding season, and flocks of 50 or more birds are not uncommon.

Mockingbird, *Mimus polyglottos.*

The mockingbird belongs to a New World family of birds whose members are noted for their ability to mimic the calls and songs of other birds; hence the family name Mimidae. In Hawaii mockingbirds have been noted to imitate parts of the calls or songs of such birds as the Golden Plover, Red-vented Bulbul, Shama Thrush, Common Myna and Cardinal. In addition to some nine species of mockingbirds, the family contains thrashers, catbirds and a bird called the Trembler that inhabits the islands of the Lesser Antilles. In much of their range in North America, the mockingbird defends a territory throughout the year, and the birds are typically belligerent to other species as well as to members of their own. Mockingbirds will attack their own images seen in windows, windshields and even shiny hubcaps of automobiles; they are noted for "dive-bombing" cats, dogs and snakes. Edward L. Caum reported: "Since 1928 a number of these birds, imported from the Mainland by private individuals, ostensibly as cage birds, have been intentionally liberated in Honolulu; from 1931 to 1933 numbers of them were brought in by the Hui Manu for liberation on Oahu, and in 1933 by the Hui Manu of Maui." There appear to be no other records of the release of mockingbirds but the species is now common on parts of Kauai, Oahu, Molokai, Lanai, Maui and Hawaii. The distribution on Oahu is spotty, being fairly common at Diamond Head, Fort Shafter, Radford Terrace and Barbers Point. On Maui the birds are found from sea level to 9,000 feet on Haleakala. The mockingbird apparently colonized Hawaii from Maui, and the species is now common in the dry kiawe habitat in the Kawaihae to Kamuela region.

Shama Thrush, *Copsychus malabaricus.*

This thrush (family Turdidae) has a wide distribution that extends from Ceylon and India to Vietnam, Laos and Java. Taxonomists recognize 17 different geographical races. "Shama" is the Hindi name for this bird. Alexander Isenberg released several Shamas on Kauai in 1931. The Hui Manu imported birds in 1940 and released them at several sites in Honolulu. The Shama is now a common species in suitable habitats on both islands. The Shama prefers areas with dense undergrowth, but it also occurs on the Manoa campus of the University of Hawaii, the Na Laau Arboretum on Diamond Head and at the Makiki nursery. Although often a shy species, Shamas are also inquisitive: They can be induced to approach an observer who imitates the bird's clear, whistlelike song. In places where the birds are accustomed to people, such as Waimea Falls Park and Paradise Park, the birds often perch on a bare branch only a few feet away. The Shama is noted for its loud, clear and melodious singing. Nests that have been found in Hawaii have been built in tree cavities, but the Shama also builds its nests in vines and shrubs. A pair on Kauai built a nest in a pair of shoes and in a woman's purse that had been hung under the eaves of a house. Clutch size in Hawaii varies from three to five eggs. Both sexes incubate the eggs and feed the young.

Japanese White-eye, *Zosterops japonicus japonicus.*

This race of the White-eye (family Zosteropidae) inhabits the main islands of Japan and the islands lying between Japan and Korea. The Japanese name is Mejiro. The first Japanese White-eyes were imported from Japan in 1929 by the Territorial Board of Agriculture and Forestry and released on Oahu. The Hui Manu imported birds and there were Mejiro clubs that held singing contests in Honolulu during this period that also brought in White-eyes. The Japanese White-eye is a remarkable example of the success of an introduced species, and now it undoubtedly is the most abundant passerine bird in the Islands. There is virtually no place that one can go without seeing these birds. They occur from sea level to tree line on Hawaii and Maui; they inhabit areas with less than 10 inches of annual rainfall and those that have 300 inches. Except during the nesting season, White-eyes usually are seen in flocks, and these typically are noisy. They have a sweet *pseet* call note, but also a harsh, scolding twitter. Their diet consists primarily of insects but includes some nectar and fruit. White-eyes sometimes join with other species to "mob" owls during the daytime. The nesting season on Oahu extends from February into August. The nest is a neat, compact structure, usually attached to at least two twigs or other supports, so that the nests are semipendant. A wide variety of materials is used, and, on the Manoa campus of the university, the lining often consists of human hair. Nests have been found in more than 50 different trees and shrubs.

Red Munia, *Amandava amandava.*

A large number of weaverbirds (family Ploceidae) have been intentionally released in the Islands, especially on Hawaii and Oahu. A number of these species belong to the subfamily Estrildinae, or waxbills. The three subspecies of the Red Munia (the Strawberry Finch in the pet store trade) are native to Pakistan, India, southern Nepal, Burma, Java and Bali. Edward Caum wrote in 1933: "It is not known with certainty when these birds came to Hawaii, but it was probably sometime between 1900 and 1910. Many were imported as cage birds during this period and it is supposed that the present population is derived from individuals escaped from captivity." This munia has been established in the Pearl Harbor region for many years, and, during the past decade, also has been seen on the Waipio Peninsula, West Beach area and at Kawainui Marsh near Kailua. Nothing has been published on the ecology or breeding biology of this species in Hawaii.

Common Indian Myna, *Acridotheres tristis tristis.*

This myna is native to Ceylon, India and adjacent regions. It also has been introduced to Malay, Natal, Seychelles, Australia and a number of islands in the Pacific Ocean. This is one of 104 species in the starling family (Sturnidae), of which the European Starling (*Sturnus vulgaris*) is a familiar bird in North America. According to Edward L. Caum, the Common Indian Myna was "introduced from India in 1865 by Dr. William Hillebrand to combat the plague of army worms that was ravaging the pasture lands of the islands." Caum gave an excellent description of this species when he wrote that it is "a perky, self-confident, pugnacious, and noisy bird, in many of its antics disconcertingly human." Mynas and other starlings are gregarious birds that feed and roost in large flocks. Many hundreds of mynas gather in favorite roosting trees at dusk in Honolulu, where the raucous calls continue as new birds arrive at the roost. The myna is common to abundant in lowland areas, and I have seen them sitting on the backs of cattle at South Point on Hawaii. They may be encountered at elevations up to at least 8,000 feet on Mauna Kea. Mynas build their nests in any nook or cranny that will hold a large pile of twigs, leaves, paper and other materials. These sites include holes in trees or buildings, traffic lights, air conditioners, ledges and palm trees. The nesting season on Oahu lasts from January through August. The eggs are immaculate blue to blue-green in color. Mynas on Oahu often are parasitized by an eye nematode, and some birds are infected with bird malaria.

Warbling Silverbill, *Lonchura malabarica cantans.*

This African seed-eater was first discovered on the island of Hawaii in 1974. A large population was found on the leeward slope of Kohala Mountain at that time, and it is assumed that this species first was released on the Puuwaawaa Ranch a decade earlier. By 1978, flocks of "hundreds of birds" were found in both North Kohala and South Kohala and birds were seen at Pohakuloa at an elevation of 6,500 feet. During December 1978, some 40 silverbills were observed in kiawe thickets below Ulupalakua, Maui, and during 1979 several birds were found on Lanai. The seed-eating habits of the silverbill will make the growing of small-grain crops impossible on the islands where it has become established. For the small size of the bird (four to 4.25 inches in total length), silverbills build large, domed nests of grasses with an entrance on one side. The nests are lined with grassheads and feathers, and often are built in kiawe trees that have no leaves at all. The breeding season lasts at least from November to April and probably much longer than that. The very small eggs are immaculate white and clutches as large as eight eggs have been found.

Susan G Monden

Spotted Munia, *Lonchura punctulata*.

This munia, also called the Ricebird, is native to Ceylon, India, Nepal, Burma, and is found southward into Malaysia and the Indo-Chinese region and the Philippines. The Ricebird was released in Hawaii by Dr. William Hillebrand about 1865. As of 1933, Edward L. Caum wrote that this species "was not particularly common in districts where rice is not grown." It was a serious pest on rice crops. Rice is no longer grown in Hawaii, but the Ricebird is now an abundant species on all of the Islands, being found in open areas wherever there are weed seeds and small-grain crops. When experimental crops of sorghum were planted in former sugar cane land during 1972, Spotted Munias and House Finches destroyed 50 tons of grain from a plot that was expected to produce 60 tons. Spotted Munias nest throughout the year in Hawaii. The large, grass nests are roughly retort-shaped; the entrance is at the end of the downward-directed neck of the nest. The eggs are immaculate white and the clutch varies from four to six eggs. Ricebirds use their old nests as dormitories and a family of birds will use an old nest for roosting for several months.

Black-headed Munia, _Lonchura malacca atricapilla_.

This subspecies is native to eastern India, Burma and northwestern Yunan. It is known also as the Chestnut Mannikin, Black-headed Nun and Black-hooded Nun. Another subspecies (_malacca_) from southern India is called the Tricolored Nun or Mannikin in the pet store trade. The Black-headed Munia was imported into Hawaii as a cage bird between 1936 and 1941. It is assumed that escaped birds established the wild population, which was first reported at West Loch, Pearl Harbor, in April 1959. An estimated 900 birds were seen in this region during 1972. No studies of this munia have been made in Hawaii, but we know that the range includes West Beach, Salt Lake and Mililani Town; one bird was collected near Laie. This species was first reported on Kauai during 1976, and it is now common between Lihue and Barking Sands. The Black-headed Munia frequents golf courses, grassy roadsides, weedy margins of cane fields and anywhere that grass seeds are available. They may flush rapidly, fly upward and then quickly drop downward into the vegetation, where it may be nearly impossible to find them. The nesting has not been described in Hawaii.

Java Sparrow, *Padda oryzivora.*

This is the Java Ricebird or Paddy Ricebird in the East. It is thought to have been endemic only to Java and Bali, but it has been introduced to many other regions, from the Philippines to Ceylon. Although this species may have been introduced about 1865 and again about 1900, these birds did not become established. The present rapidly expanding population probably derived from cage birds that were intentionally released on Diamond Head after 1965. One pair raised young there during the winter of 1968. The increase in numbers since that time has been phenomenal. Java Sparrows now occur from Kahala to Tripler Hospital, with occasional sightings on the Windward side of Oahu (Bellows Field, Kailua and Kaneohe). On Oahu the Java Sparrow begins its nesting season by October, when the day lengths are growing shorter. The birds build nests in tree cavities, in palm trees, under the eaves of buildings, horizontal pipes and other artificial crannies. The eggs are white.

Saffron Finch, *Sicalis flaveola.* (Opposite.)

This finch (family Fringillidae) is native to South America, where it occurs in all countries except Chile. It has been introduced in Jamaica and the Panama Canal Zone. It is assumed that these birds were intentionally released on the slopes of Diamond Head, where it was first reported in October 1965. Saffron Finches now occur in the Diamond Head-Kapiolani Park region, Radford Terrace and Salt Lake; one or two birds have been reported also in widely scattered areas of Oahu. The Saffron Finch is established on Hawaii, from Kawaihae to the Puuwaawaa Ranch. The breeding biology of the Saffron Finch has not been studied in its native range, but there it is said to be a cavity nester. The first nest found in Hawaii in 1977, however, was cup-shaped and built about eight feet from the ground in an Alexandrian laurel of twigs, rootlets, weed stems and leaves. The two eggs had a background color of grayish-white, with reddish-brown spots scattered over the shell and with a concentration around the larger end of the egg. The incubation period at this nest was 13 days.

Red-crested Cardinal, *Paroaria coronata*. (See next page.)

This species long was called the Brazilian Cardinal in Hawaii, but it is native also to Uruguay, Paraguay, eastern Bolivia and northern Argentina. This species was first released on Oahu during 1928, with further releases being made during the following three years. The Red-crested Cardinal is now a very common species on Oahu. Although there appear to be no records of its introduction on the other islands, this cardinal is increasing its range on Kauai, is found in the Kona area of Hawaii, occurs on Molokai, and single birds were seen at two different places on Lanai in 1976. The Red-crested Cardinal has a much softer, more melodious song than that of the Cardinal. One description is *wheet-cheer-up*. During the breeding season, it is one of the first birds to sing in the morning well before daylight. The breeding season lasts from mid-December at least into September. The nests are built in a

variety of trees (such as monkeypod, shower tree, pink tecoma, mango, paperbark) often 25 or more feet from the ground. The eggs have a greenish-white background color, heavily covered with dark brown spots. The clutch usually contains two or three eggs, rarely four. The adult male and female have identical plumage; the immature birds have a brown head. Red-crested Cardinals form flocks after the nesting season is over, containing as many as 50 birds.

Yellow-billed Cardinal, *Paroaria capitata*.

This South American species is one of the latest successful introductions, being first reported in the Kailua-Kona region of Hawaii during 1973. There is no information on the source of these birds. The birds may be seen at Pu'uhonua O Honaunau (Place of Refuge), Opaeula and Aimakapa ponds, and Honokohau boat harbor. Nests have been found in May and brown-headed immature birds in March and July.

Yellow-fronted Canary, *Serinus mozambicus.*

This species, native to a large part of Africa, is known as the Green Singing Finch in the pet store trade. This canary is kept as a cage bird by the native peoples of Africa, who trap them in double cages containing decoy birds. The Yellow-fronted Canary was first reported on Oahu in 1964 when one bird was seen at Koko Head. One bird was seen on Diamond Head in 1965 and one year later 17 birds were counted there during the annual Christmas count of the Hawaii Audubon Society. This is now a common resident in the Diamond Head-Kapiolani Park region and birds have been seen at Kawela Bay near the Kuilima Hotel, some 30 miles north of Diamond Head. Although probably released on the Puuwaawaa Ranch on Hawaii some 20 years ago, the Yellow-fronted Canary was not reported on that island until 1978, when a flock of 11 birds was seen in the mamane-naio forest on Mauna Kea. Since that time, large numbers have been seen on Hualalai and the species has been observed at Halepohaku at an elevation of 9,200 feet on Mauna Kea, and in the ohia forests along Stainback Highway on Mauna Loa. On Oahu, the Yellow-fronted Canary begins its nesting season during October. The nest is a very neat, compact structure, composed primarily of fine grasses but covered on the outside with cotton. The two eggs in a clutch are immaculate white in color. The Yellow-fronted Canary is closely related to the familiar canary (*Serinus canaria*), which occurs as a wild species on Madeira, the Azores and Canary Islands. Domestic canaries were released on Midway Atoll in 1910, and a wild population still survives there.

House Finch, *Carpodacus mexicanus frontalis.*

This finch has a wide distribution in western North America from British Columbia southward into Mexico. The House Finch is now also established in New York, Connecticut and Massachusetts from cage birds that were released on Long Island. The House Finch was brought from California and released in Hawaii "prior to 1870." It is now very common on all Islands, in residential and urban areas, in both wet and dry rural regions, and in the high ranch and forest lands of Hawaii and Maui. Males in Hawaii are noted for the wide variation in their plumage, some being brightly colored like Mainland males and others having the red colors replaced by yellowish or orange-red patches. Because of their fondness for papaya, the bird is called the Papayabird in Hawaii. Despite this liking of papaya and some other soft fruits, the House Finch is primarily a seedeater, frequently also eating flower buds. Their destruction of the experimental sorghum crops already has been mentioned. The nesting season in Hawaii begins in mid-February and lasts into September. Pandanus and palm trees are favorite nesting trees. The clutch in Hawaii varies from three to five eggs. House Finches are unusual among passerine birds in that the adults do not remove all of the fecal sacs after the first few days of the nestling period, so that these sacs accumulate on the rim of the nest before the young fledge.

Table 1
EXTINCT HAWAIIAN BIRDS

Full Species

Laysan Rail, *Porzana palmeri*
Hawaiian Rail, *Porzana sandwichensis*
Oahu 'Ō'ō, *Moho apicalis*
Molokai 'Ō'ō, *Moho bishopi*
Black Mamo, *Drepanis funerea*
(Molokai)
Kioea, *Chaetoptila angustipluma*
(Hawaii)
Hawaii 'Ō'ō, *Moho nobilis*
Greater 'Amakihi, *Hemignathus*
sagittirostris (Hawaii)
Greater Koa Finch, *Rhodacanthis*
palmeri (Hawaii)
Lesser Koa Finch, *Rhodacanthis*
flaviceps (Hawaii)
Kona Grosbeak, *Chloridops kona*
(Hawaii)
'Ula-'Ai-Hāwane, *Ciridops anna*
(Hawaii)
Mamo, *Drepanis pacifica* (Hawaii)
'Akialoa, *Hemignathus obscurus*
(all three subspecies are extinct:
Oahu, Lanai and Hawaii)

Subspecies

Laysan Millerbird, *Acrocephalus*
f. familiaris
Laysan Honeycreeper, *Himatione*
sanguinea freethii
Oahu Thrush, *Phaeornis obscurus*
oahensis
Oahu 'Ākepa, *Loxops coccineus rufus*
Oahu Nukupu'u, *Hemignathus l. lucidus*
Lanai Thrush, *Phaeornis obscurus*
lanaiensis
Lanai Creeper, *Paroreomyza montana*

Extinct Populations of Surviving Species*

'I'iwi, *Vestiaria coccinea* on Lanai
'Ō'ū, *Psittirostra psittacea,* on Oahu,
Molokai and Lanai
Crested Honeycreeper, *Palmeria dolei,*
on Molokai

---

*Species extinct on one island but
surviving on another.

Table 2

RARE AND ENDANGERED HAWAIIAN LAND BIRDS

Hawaiian Hawk, *Buteo solitarius*
Hawaiian Crow, *Corvus hawaiiensis*
Small Kauai Thrush, *Phaeornis palmeri*
Large Kauai Thrush, *Phaeornis obscurus myadestina*
Molokai Thrush, *Phaeornis o. rutha*
Nihoa Millerbird, *Acrocephalus familiaris kingi*
Kauai 'Ō'ō, *Moho braccatus*
Kauai Nukupu'u, *Hemignathus lucidus hanapepe*
Kauai 'Akialoa, *Hemignathus procerus*
Kauai 'Ō'u, *Psittirostra psittacea*
Oahu Creeper, *Paroreomyza maculata*
Oahu 'I'iwi, *Vestiaria coccinea*
Molokai Creeper, *Paroreomyza flammea*
Molokai 'I'iwi, *Vestiaria coccinea*
Lanai 'Apapane, *Himatione s. sanguinea*

Lanai 'Amakihi, *Hemignathus virens wilsoni*
Maui 'Ākepa, *Loxops coccineus ochraceus*
Maui Crested Honeycreeper, *Palmeria dolei*
Maui Nukupu'u, *Hemignathus lucidus affinis*
Maui Parrotbill, *Pseudonestor xanthophrys*
Maui 'Ō'ū, *Psittirostra psittacea*
Hawaii 'Ō'ū, *Psittirostra psittacea*
Hawaii Creeper, *Oreomystis mana*
Hawaii 'Ākepa, *Loxops c. coccineus*
'Akiapola'au, *Hemignathus munroi*
Palila, *Loxioides bailleui*
Laysan Finch, *Telespyza cantans*
Nihoa Finch, *Telespyza ultima*
Po'o Uli, *Melamprosops phaeosoma*